Bilingual Reading Program

Non-fiction
English and Chinese

从茶叶到茶

From Tea Leaves to Tea

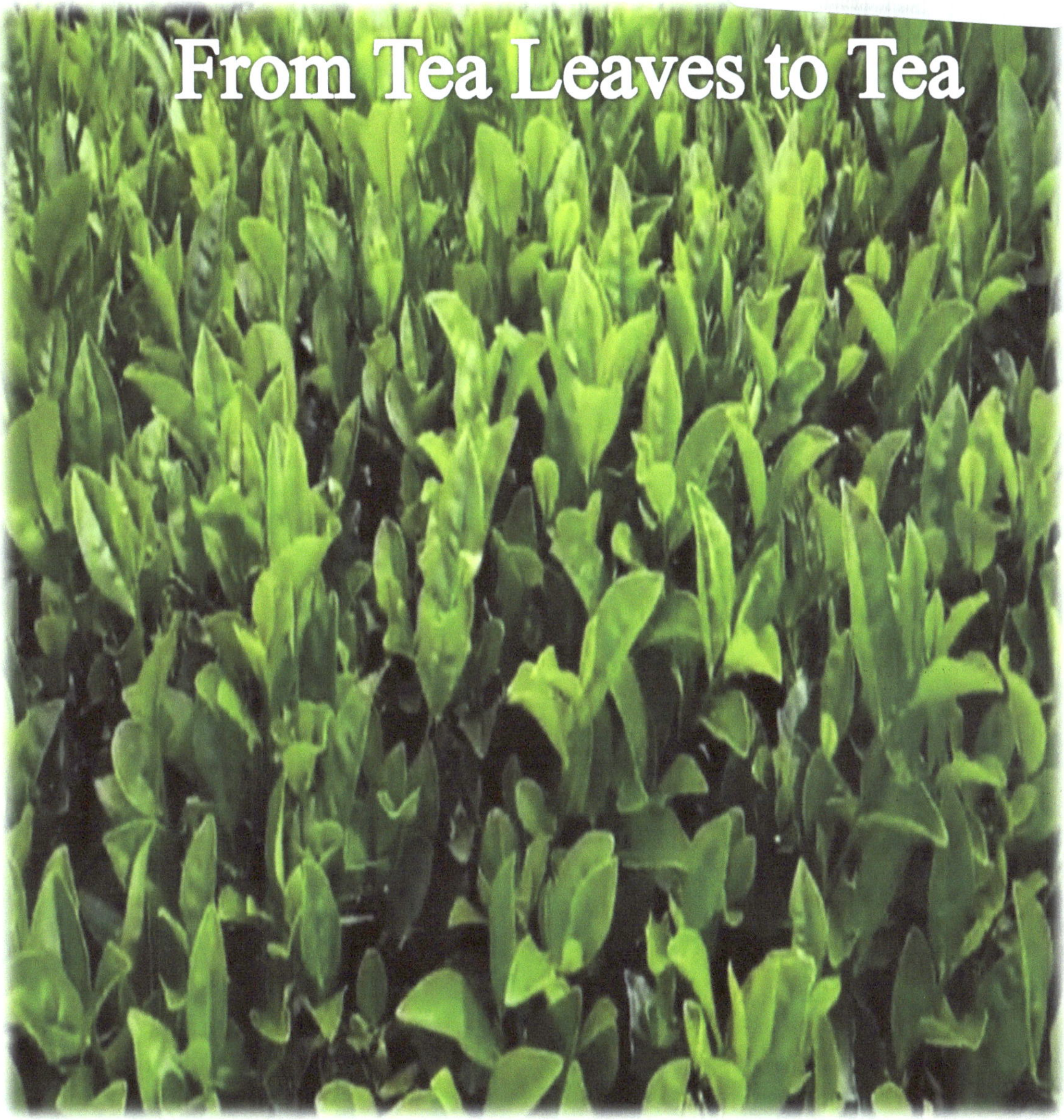

Text copyright @2020 by Mei Lan Wang
All rights reserved.
Published by EduOrchids Inc.
Bilingual Reading Program
First Printed in January, 2020

ISBN: 9-781999-285807

Acknowledgement

Most of the pictures
in this book
are provided by
Insantulo Tea Co. Ltd.
Nanjing, Fujian, China.

致谢

此书中的大部分照片由
南靖印象土楼茶叶有限公司
提供

To: Zhuo and Yue

    for their continuous efforts!

致：卓,越

    感谢他们不懈的努力！

Bilingual Reading Program

From Tea Leaves to Tea

从茶叶到茶

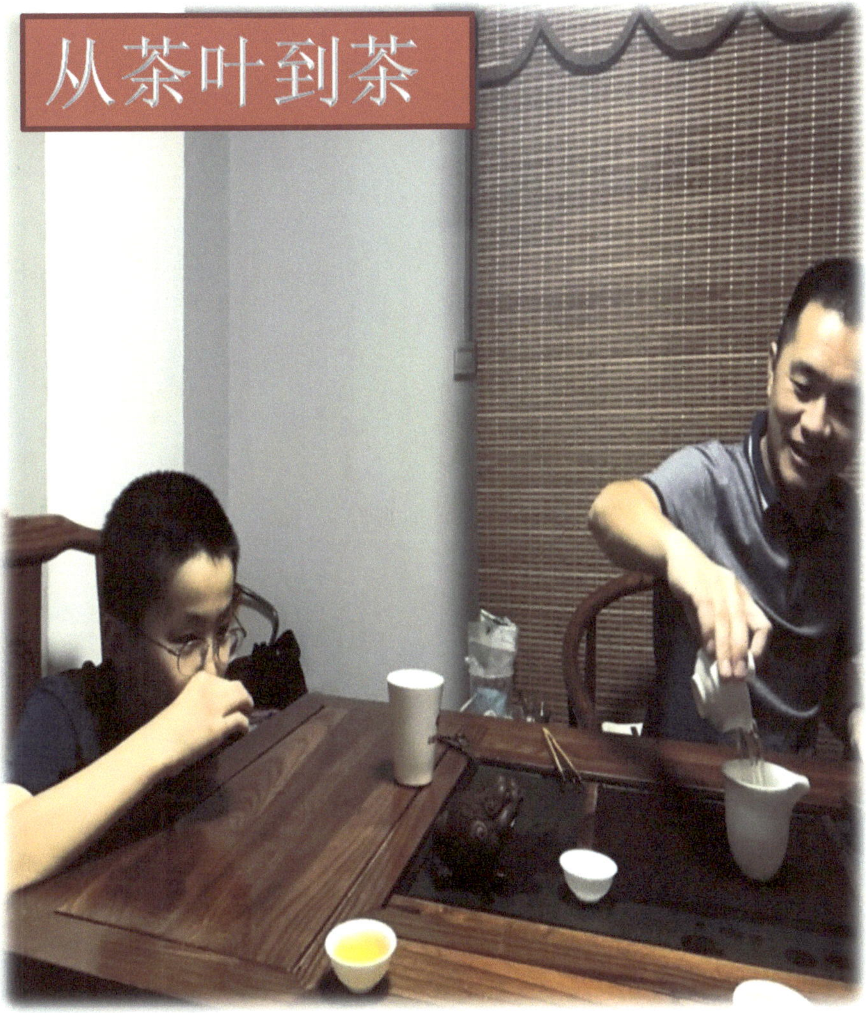

Written by Mei Lan Wang 王梅兰

EduOrchids Inc.

Toronto   Xiamen

Look!
There are rows and
rows of tea plants
on the mountains.

看!
山上长着
一排排的茶树。

This is a tea plantation in my hometown, Nanjing, Fujian, China.

我的家乡在中国福建南靖。
这是家乡的一个茶园。

The new tender leaves
are growing.
It's time to pick
the tea leaves.

新的嫩叶
正茁壮成长。
采茶的季节到了。

The workers are
busy picking tea leaves.
These tea plants
are still small.
The workers can
sit while picking leaves.

工人们
正忙着采茶。
这些茶树
还很矮。
工人们可以
坐着采茶。

These tea plants
are much bigger.
The workers have to stand
while picking tea leaves.

这些茶树
高多了。
工人们只能站着
采茶了。

Tea Plants

茶树

Some workers use bags
to collect the tea leaves.
Others wear bamboo
baskets around
their waists
to collect the leaves.

有的工人用袋子
收集采下的茶叶。
另一些工人则是
腰系竹篓
来收集采下的茶叶。

The workers
spread the tea leaves
onto the bamboo trays.
The bamboo trays
with tea leaves
are placed on
the cement ground.

工人们
把茶叶
铺在竹簸箕上。
再把装着茶叶的
竹簸箕
摆在
水泥场上。

On sunny days,
these tea leaves
are left in the sun
for the whole day.

天晴的日子，
这些茶叶
在阳光下
暴晒一天。

At the end of the day, the workers collect all the tea leaves. Then they put them into some deeper bamboo trays.

傍晚时,
工人们就把茶叶
收起来。
然后,他们把茶叶
放到深一点的簸箕里。

Next, they place
the sun-dried leaves
into a roller
to make them dryer
and softer.

然后，工人们把晒过的
茶叶放到
圆筒里摇青，
让茶叶更加收水，柔软。

After that, the tea leaves
are put into another kind
of machine to tumble dry.
Then, the workers
use their hands
to rub those tea leaves.

接下来,这些茶叶
被放进另一种工具里
进行滚炒。
然后,工人们
再用双手
揉搓茶叶,炒青。

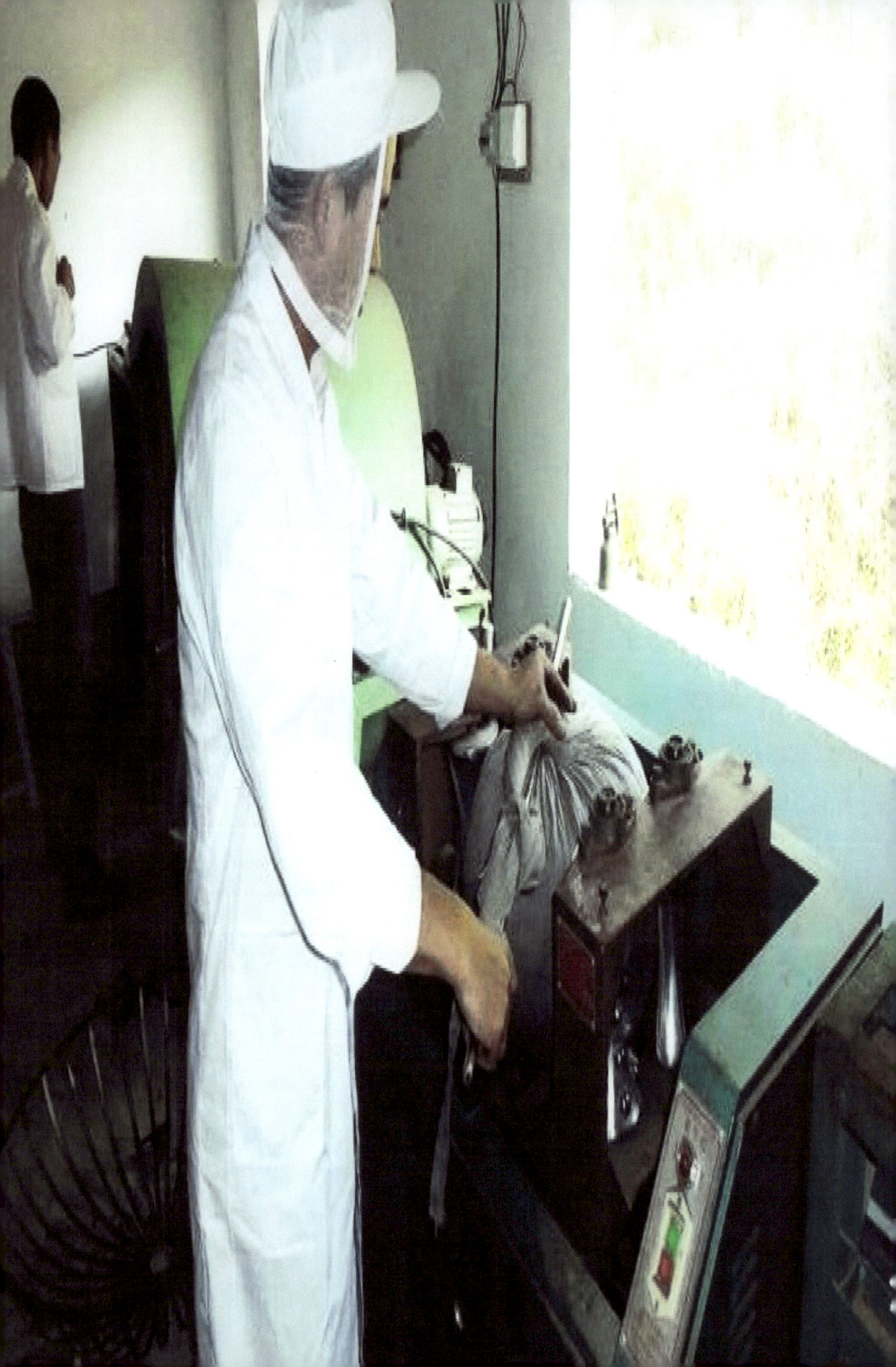

This worker is kneading and twisting the tea leaves. This step decides the shape of the tea products.

这个工人正在揉捻叶青。
这道工序决定了
茶叶成品的形状。

The twisted tea leaves
are spread
on the bamboo trays.
This worker is putting
the trays in the special
oven for baking.

揉捻过的叶青
被放到
簸箕上。
这个工人正把装茶叶的簸箕
放到特殊的烤炉里
进行烘培。

After baking,
the tea leaves are
spread onto the table.
The workers begin to
hand-pick
the hard leaf stems.

烘培完后，
茶叶成品摊开
铺放在桌子上。
工人们开始用手
挑捡
那些硬的茶梗。

Here comes the machine for tea packaging.
The tea leaves are then packed into mini bags.

这是茶叶包装机器。
茶叶被装入
一个个小袋子里。

The last step is to label each mini package.

最后，每个小包装都贴上商标。

In my hometown,
there are many different
types of tea.
People can buy
their favourite tea products.

在我的家乡，
茶叶品种繁多。
人们可以
买到他们最喜欢的茶叶。

Time to enjoy
a nice cup of tea!
Mmmmm…..
What a nice flavour
of hometown!

好好地品一下茶!
茶香四溢...
多好的家乡味啊!

Vocabulary	词汇
tea	茶
leaves	叶子
tea plant	茶树
bamboo basket	竹篓
tea pot	茶壶
worker	工人
dry	晒干
pick	采，摘
make tea	泡茶
drink	喝，品

Non-fiction Photo Story
Bilingual Reading Program
For Grades K-3
English and Chinese Vocabulary

Copyright © 2019 Mei Lan Wang

www.eduorchids.com

ISBN 9-781999-285807

USA $ 12.99 CAD $ 16.99

www.ingramcontent.com/pod-product-compliance
Lightning Source LLC
LaVergne TN
LVHW072054070426
835508LV00002B/90